Mathematical Reasoning

FOR SELECTIVE SCHOOL TESTS, OPPORTUNITY CLASS TESTS AND PROBLEM SOLVING

BOOK 1

Mohan Dhall

Five Senses Education Pty Ltd
2/195 Prospect Highway
Seven Hills 2147
New South Wales
Australia

First Published 2021

Dhall, Mohan
Mathematical Reasoning – Book 1

ISBN 978-1-76032-380-6

Contents

Foreword	iv
Mathematical reasoning – an Introduction	1
Mathematical Reasoning Problems	3
Answers	31
Summary of Answers	32
Fully Worked Solutions	33
Multiple Choice Answer Sheets	55

Foreword

Mathematical reasoning skills are an aspect of critical thinking. Critical thinking is an essential skill that students need to develop. Mathematical reasoning requires students to be able to work numerically, understand number relationships, understand mathematical operations, see patterns, transpose, extrapolate, do graphical interpretation, understand data represented in concrete and abstract forms, understand spatial relationships and representations, calculate the probability of an event or events occurring, and use known data to calculate unknown data.

Developing mathematical reasoning is necessary for making informed decisions in everyday life: comparing prices of packages with different weights, understanding weights and measurements when mixing food, or understanding ratios and volumes when mixing paint and colour.

In a rapidly changing world, characterised by multiple and competing information sources, developing mathematical reasoning skills and the ability to reason logically has never been more important. Mathematical reasoning is a fundamental life skill for a meaningful life.

Practice on the problems in this book will help students to develop a range of mathematical reasoning skills. Prior to practicing, students should read through the section at the start which provides strategies. Using these strategies will be helpful to developing the skills required to think through complex problems.

The author would like to acknowledge Michael McKay who assisted with editing.

About the author

Mohan Dhall is an experienced teacher and teacher-educator, author and educational manager. Trained in gifted education, Mohan has developed many critical thinking courses for students and has also trained teachers in critical and creative thinking skills. As Director, he ran one of Australia's longest running school based centres for gifted children. He has written hundreds of different types of critical thinking questions and had more than 70 books published. Mohan is currently the Academic Leader of M2K Education and Advisory.

Mathematical reasoning - an introduction

Mathematical reasoning involves the application and the development of a number of different thinking skills. Aspects of critical thinking include skills involving each of the following:

- Analysis
- Comparing
- Generalising
- Estimation
- Justification
- Grouping and ordering
- Abstracting
- Adding, subtracting, multiplying and dividing
- Identifying patterns and numerical relationships
- Understanding symbolic representations
- Explaining
- Describing
- Identifying

An essential aspect of mathematical reasoning is logic. Logic is an application of the principles of reasoning to evidence or data. Two important aspects of logical reasoning are deductive reasoning and inductive reasoning.

Deductive reasoning

This type of thinking requires a person to be able to draw valid or certain conclusion from a premise or premises and the application of defined rules.

Inductive reasoning

This type of thinking requires a person to be able to draw general conclusions from the premises but may not be certain. The generalisation should be plausible, but it will not be certain.

Students may find that they are distracted by generalisation that are plausible but are not assured.

General strategies for dealing with different questions

When presented with mathematical information, rules and data it is important to keep a clear mind about what the problem requires and what information, facts and relationships have been given. A strategy for dealing with complicated information is to write down, in shortened notation, what has been given.

Other strategies include:

1. Reading ALL of the information provided before answering the question.
2. If there is information given in bullet points – such as Statements – then as you read each statement as yourself, "is this true? Does this make sense?"
3. Read ALL of the answers before making a selection.
4. Even if you think the answer is A or B complete reading ALL of the answers prior to making your selection.
5. If there is graphical data, look at the title of the graph, and the label on each axis before you start your analysis. Carefully look at the scale as well so you know what the values represented are. Note that a graph can have three axes (left, right and horizontal).
6. Be prepared to keep more than one piece of information in your mind at a time. You will need to do this when there are different rules given to information.
7. DO NOT use your general knowledge to answer any of the questions. All the information you need is in the question. No extraneous information should be required to successfully answer the questions.
8. Identify the type of question being asked so that you know what thinking skills you will be utilising.
9. If there is visual stimulus look at it carefully and try and determine the relationships between the relevant parts of the stimulus.
10. Use estimation as a time saver. Often a quick estimation will help.
11. If you do not 'see information' then practice reading to yourself out loud. You can also underline key words in data to retain it.
12. There can be two or three steps required so make sure you complete a question to the end, not answering it before the final calculation has been made.
13. If you are unsure, experiment. It is okay to try a few combinations as you work your way through a mathematical problem. Baulking and giving up does not solve problems or create resilience.

Mathematical Reasoning Problems

Question 1

Davo's watch reads 21:48.

What is the time three quarters of an hour later, in 12-hour format?

A 10:23 am

B 10:33 am

C 8:23 pm

D 10:33 pm

E 9:33 pm

Question 2

Josephine divides a white piece of paper into equal sections. She colours some sections yellow, as shown.

Josephine then colours $\frac{2}{3}$ of the whole paper blue.

Finally, she colours the rest of the paper red.

How many sections does she colour red?

A 1

B 2

C 3

D 4

E 5

Question 3

Serena multiplies the smallest four-digit whole number by the largest four-digit whole number.

However, she makes a mistake and misses a digit from one or both whole numbers.

Which is an answer Serena cannot get?

A 0

B 99 990

C 99 900

D 999 900

E 999 000

Question 4

Ahmed is trying to calculate how fast the car is travelling. However, the speedometer has no numbers.

He knows that the maximum speed would be 210 kilometres per hour.

What is the current speed?

A 55 km per hour

B 75 km per hour

C 83 km per hour

D 90 km per hour

E 97 km per hour

Question 5

Almira is shopping online at Fash. She is based in Sydney and the online store is based in Los Angeles. There is a 17-hour time difference with Los Angeles being behind Sydney. The business advertises a 10-hour sale on Tuesday 1st March, commencing at 8am.

If it takes 10 minutes to complete a purchase and only completed purchase get the sales prices, when can Almira shop until?

A Tuesday 1st March 12.50am

B Wednesday 2nd March 12.50am

C Wednesday 2nd March 9.50am

D Wednesday 2nd March 10.50am

E Tuesday 1st March 5.50pm

Question 6

$30

$51

$47

$?

A $59

B $61

C $63

D $64

E $67

Question 7

On the five-dollar notes from a nation called Dolma there is a security code in the top left-hand corner. In this code the 5th and 6th letters from the left indicate the year and month consecutively that the note was printed.

The years start with the letter A being 2010, B being 2011 and so on.

The months are also in the order A = January, B = February and so on.

When was this note made?

A January 2015

B February 2018

C February 2107

D February 2014

E February 2015

Question 8

On a digital display the letters: B, E, S, I and O can be written numerically as 8, 3, 5 or 2, 1 and 0. For example the numbers 8, 3 and 5 can be used to make the word BEES:

Other numbers such as 7 can be L and 6 can be g.

Which of the following words cannot be made on this display?

A bless

B held

C gels

D shell

E loose

Question 9

Clare and Teresa each think of a different whole number that is greater than zero and less than 100.

- Clare's number is an even multiple of 3
- Teresa's number is an even number which is a multiple of 13.

What is the greatest difference between the largest value of Clare's number and the smallest value of Teresa's number?

A 86

B 77

C 70

D 63

E 47

Question 10

In the diagrams below A and B are squares. These shapes have the same area. What is the length of the side of square A?

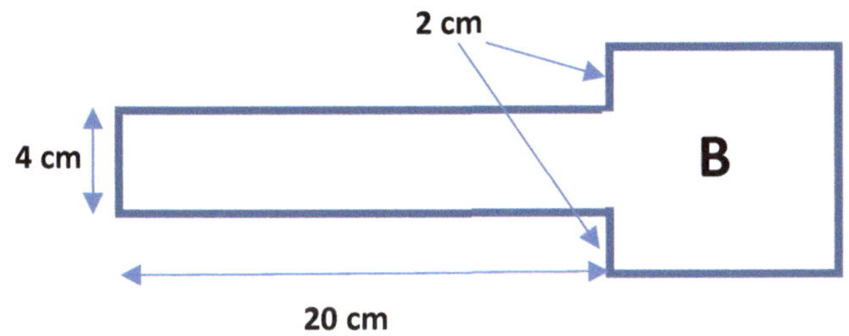

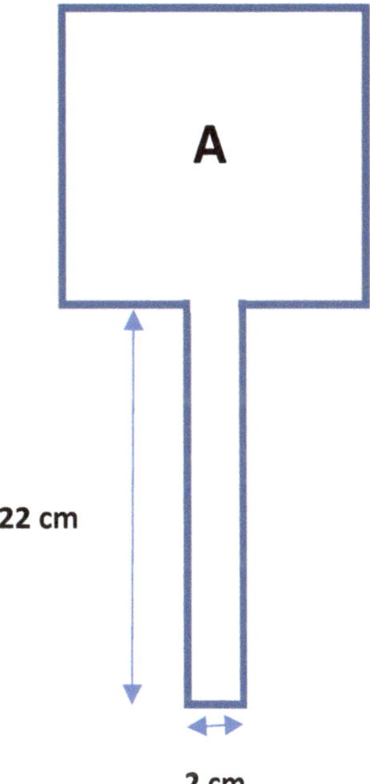

A 10 cm

B 14 cm

C 12 cm

D 8 cm

E 11 cm

Question 11

Jessie and Joshua see this number: 12 430 000.

Joshua rounds the number to the nearest million, but Jessie rounds the number to the nearest hundred thousand.

How different are their answers?

- **A** 0
- **B** 20 000
- **C** 60 000
- **D** 200 000
- **E** 400 000

Question 12

In a 'magic square', each row, each column and each diagonal add up to the same total. In the magic square below, some of the numbers are missing.

22		★
21		
26		**24**

What is the value of ★?

- **A** 27
- **B** 25
- **C** 23
- **D** 20
- **E** 19

Question 13

The relationship between the weights of various objects is shown below.

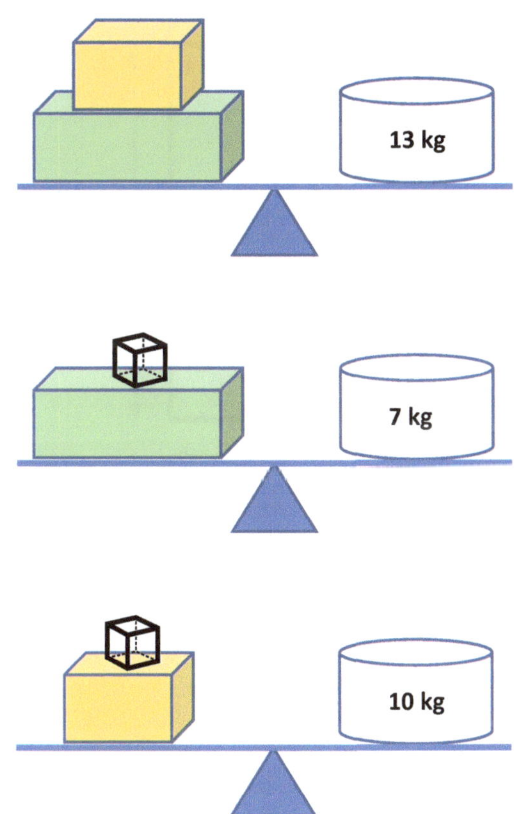

What is the weight of this arrangement?

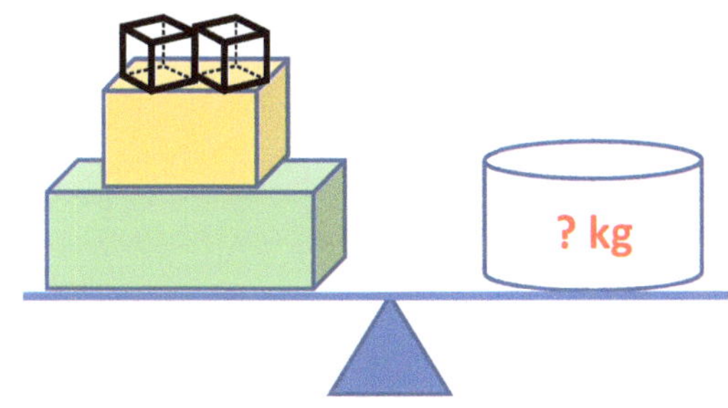

A 30 kg

B 21 kg

C 19 kg

D 18 kg

E 17 kg

Question 14

Shape Y has the same perimeter as shape X. All corners are right angles.

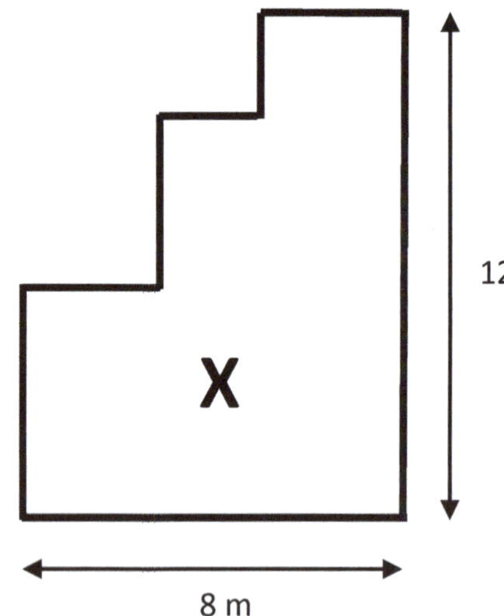

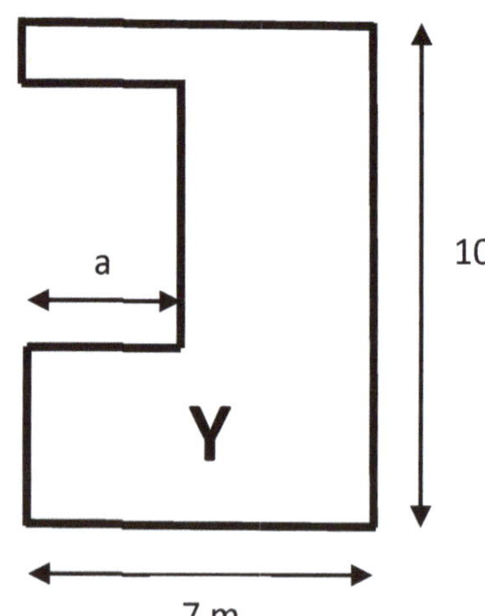

What is the value of a?

A 12 m

B 1.5 m

C 600 cm

D 300 cm

E 1.5 m

Question 15

At school Minnie's teacher has a chart. She gives stickers to the students if they do things like tidy up or help others.

The stickers are worth a certain fixed number of points.

If a person gets 3 heart stickers and 2 star stickers they get 22 points.

= 22

If a person gets 6 heart stickers and 5 star stickers they get 46 points.

= 46

What is the value of 2 heart stickers and 2 star stickers?

A 24 points

B 8 points

C 16 points

D 10 points

E 12 points

Question 16

Bernard makes a number pattern where he writes down 4 numbers. After that, every number is the sum of the previous 4 numbers. He writes this:

1 5 A 2 B 21 C

What is the value of C?

A 37

B 35

C 43

D 38

E 40

Question 17

How many whole numbers between 1 and 150 are multiples of 7, but are NOT multiples of 3, 5 or 8?

A 7

B 9

C 8

D 6

E 11

Question 18

How many faces, vertices and edges does a heptagonal prism have?

A 14

B 23

C 29

D 42

E 44

Question 19

For a party Gary buys 6 little cakes.

Josie eats $1\frac{1}{6}$

Mark eats $1\frac{1}{4}$

Edith eats $1\frac{2}{9}$

Clancy eats $\frac{3}{4}$

How much is left for Gary to eat?

A $1\frac{1}{6}$

B $1\frac{2}{9}$

C $1\frac{13}{18}$

D $1\frac{11}{18}$

E $4\frac{7}{18}$

Question 20

Bao has spinner which is divided into 8 segments.

She spins the spinner, and it points to a number 1 as shown below.

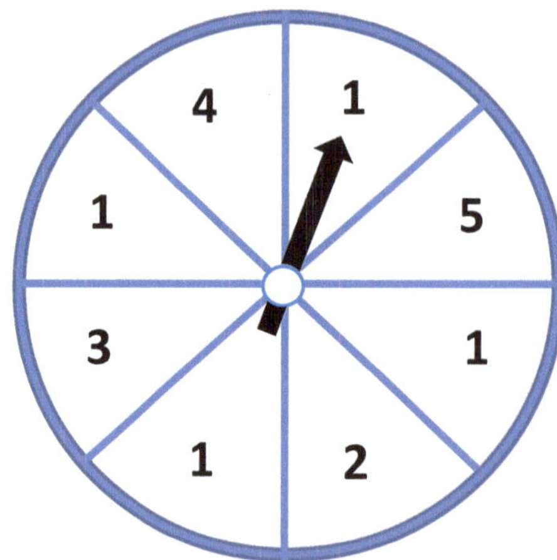

Her friend Huyen then spins the spinner.

What is the chance of Huyen getting a number which when added to Bao's number gives an answer greater than 2?

A $\frac{1}{2}$

B $\frac{3}{8}$

C $\frac{5}{8}$

D $\frac{1}{8}$

E $\frac{3}{4}$

Question 21

The graph below shows the dive that Angie took.

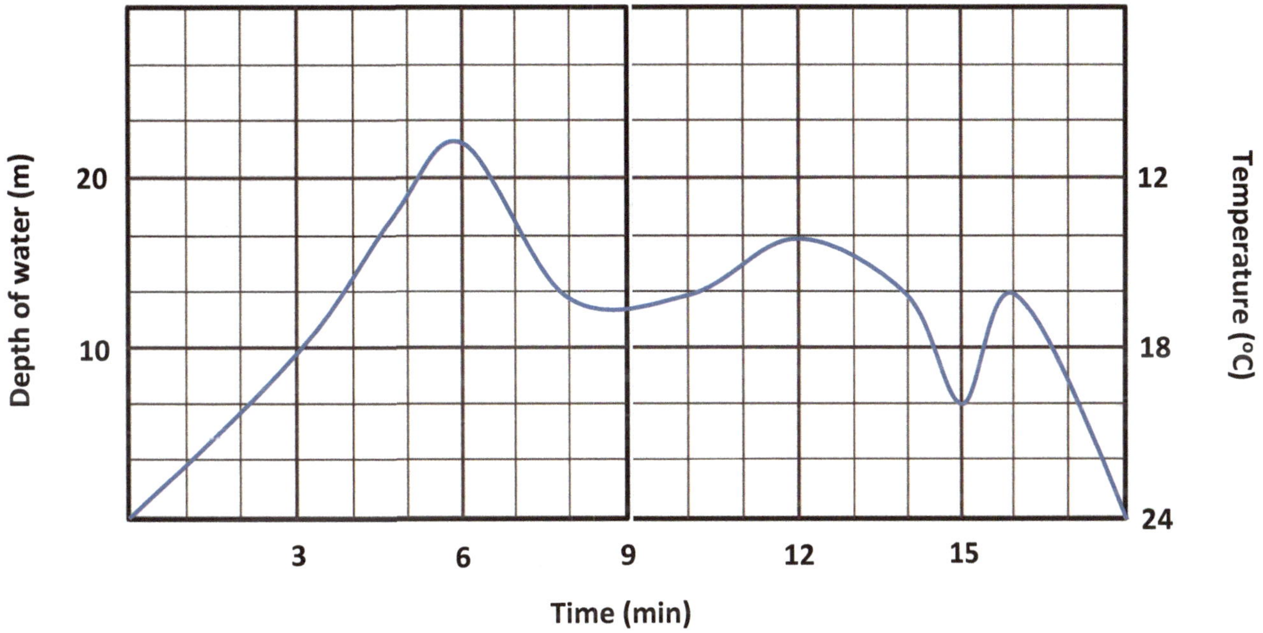

Statement 1 Angie went more than 13 metres under the surface of the water 3 times

Statement 2 Angie experienced a water temperature of 14 degrees 3 times

Statement 3 Angie spent most of her time less than 11 metres below the water's surface

Which of the following is true?

A Statement 1 and Statement 3 only

B Statement 1 and Statement 2 only

C Statement 3 only

D Statement 2 only

E Statement 1 only

Question 22

Yari wants to make a shape that has TWO axes of symmetry – one vertical and one horizontal – by adding squares to the shape below

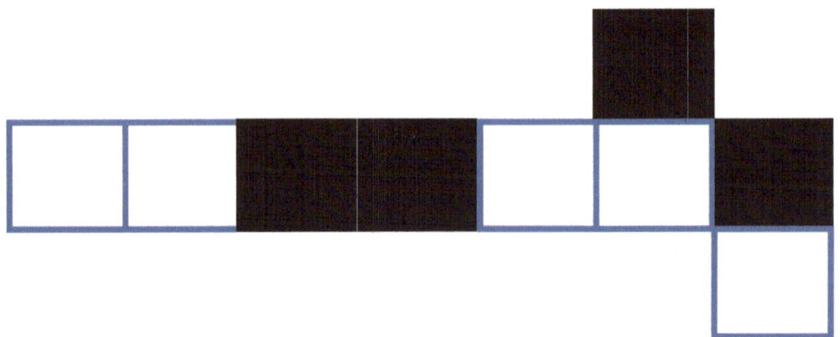

Statement 1 2 black squares are required

Statement 2 1 white square is required

Statement 3 3 white squares are required

Statement 4 4 black squares are required

Which of the following is correct?

A Statement 1 and Statement 2 only

B Statement 1 and Statement 3 only

C Statement 3 and Statement 4 only

D Statement 2 and Statement 4 only

E None of the statements

Question 23

Eight text messages are sent to each of 15 people. Four of those people forward six of the messages to two other people.

Which number sentence shows this information?

A (8 × 15) + (15 × 6) × 2

B 8 × (15 + 6) × 4

C 8 × 15 – 11 × 6 × 2

D 15 × (8 + 4) × 6 × 2

E (15 × 8) + (6 × 4) × 2

Question 24

The rectangle and the square have the same area.

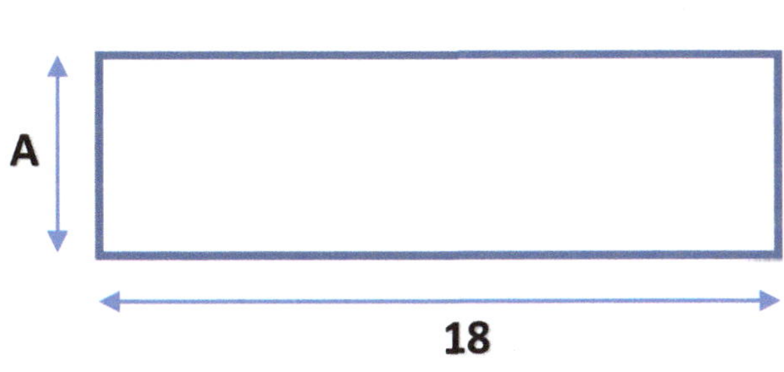

What is the value of A?

A 6 m

B 7 m

C 8 m

D 10 m

E 12 m

Question 25

A 2 litre bottle of orange juice contains 600 mL of juice. Supriya adds a two-thirds of a small jug of water to the orange juice. The jug contains 600 mL when full. Supriya drinks 540 mL of the combined juice and water and pours half of the rest into another bottle.

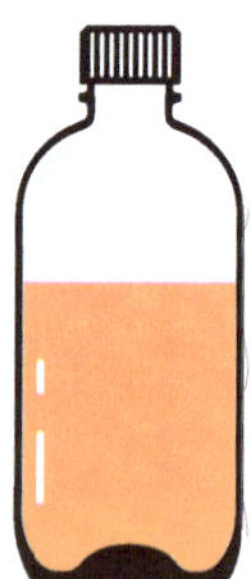

How much liquid is in the bottle?

A 1 L

B 460 mL

C 400 mL

D 230 mL

E 200 mL

Question 26

 Represents a number

 Represents a different number

× 13 = 104

\+ + = 22

What is the value of ?

A 7

B 6

C 9

D 8

E 11

Question 27

Lily had $14. She was given some money from Luisa. She then gave quarter of her money to Belinda. Belinda spent a quarter of this money and had $4.50 left.

How much did Lily give to Belinda?

A $24.00

B $12.00

C $10.00

D $9.00

E $6.00

Question 28

In a warehouse there is a large box of coloured tee-shirts each in its own bag. 

Jay knows that there are five times as many blue shirts as white shirts. She also knows that there are orange shirts, purple shirts and a black shirt.

The chances of Jay picking up an orange shirt is 0.2

Her chances of picking a purple shirt are 0.15

If there are 20 shirts in the box, how many are white?

A 1

B 2

C 4

D 5

E 8

Question 29

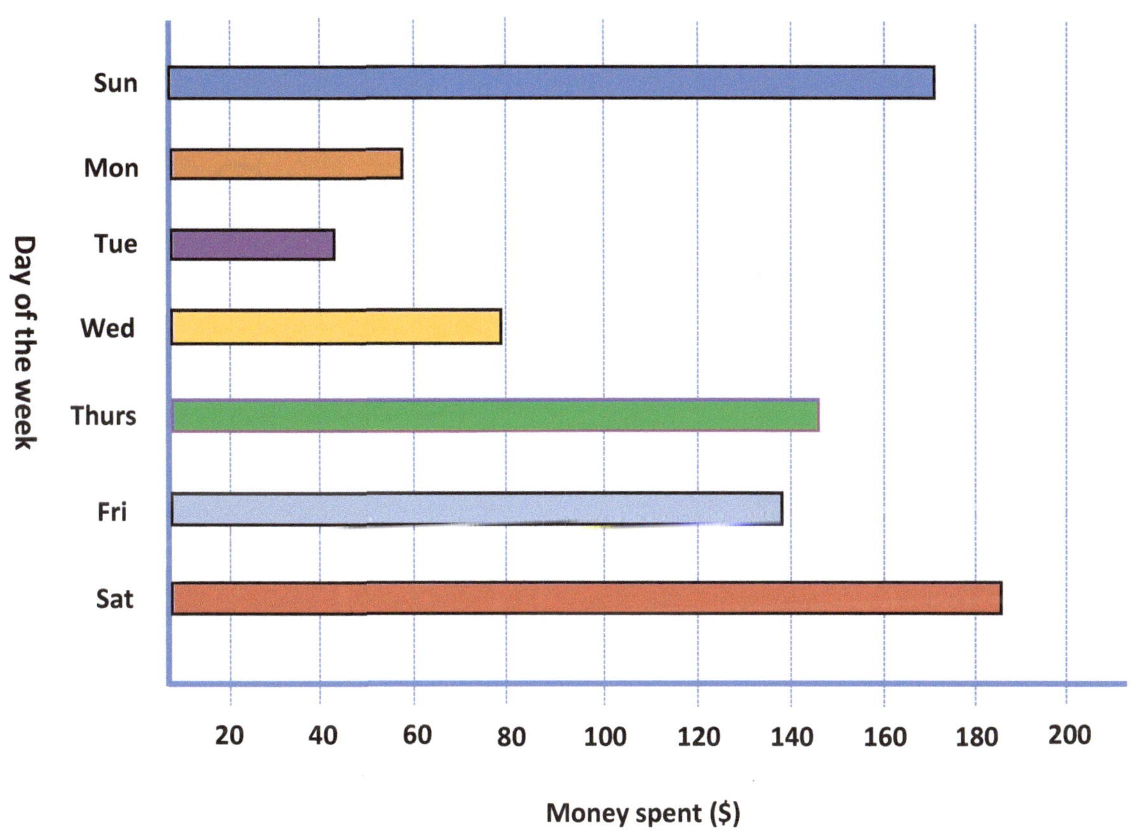

Here are three statements about the graph.

Statement 1 On average people spent twice as much on Thursday than on Wednesday.

Statement 2 The average spending on Sunday is four times the average Tuesday spending.

Statement 3 The average weekend spending is greater than the all the other days together.

Which of the following is true?

A Statement 1 only

B Statement 2 only

C Statement 3 only

D Statement 2 and 3 only

E Statement 1 and 2 only

Question 30

Jake shares a long loaf of garlic bread with 4 friends.

He gives $\frac{1}{3}$ of the slices to Andrew.

He gives 2 slices to Chan.

He gives $\frac{1}{6}$ of the loaf to Boris.

He gives 2 slices to Darcy.

Jake eats the last five slices.

How many slices did Boris eat?

A 9

B 6

C 3

D 2

E 1

Question 31

A is a white square within a black rectangle. The dimensions of the rectangle are shown. A white rectangle as well as the square are cut out of the black rectangle.

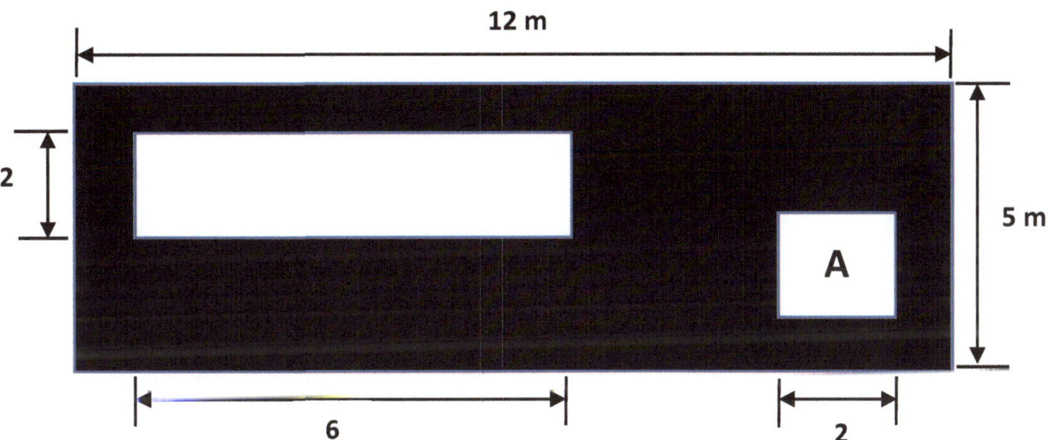

What area of the black rectangle remains after the white pieces are removed?

- **A** 60 m^2
- **B** 56 m^2
- **C** 48 m^2
- **D** 44 m^2
- **E** 36 m^2

Question 32

Queenie is using this jug to create a new juice mix. She is using the scale on the right-hand side ONLY.

She fills the jug to 75 mL of lemon juice. She then adds water taking the mix to 325 mL. She then adds orange juice to bring it to the fourth line from the top of the scale.

She pours half of this mix into a glass.

How much orange juice is in the glass?

A 50 mL

B 75 mL

C 125 mL

D 250 mL

E 450 mL

Question 33

The diagram below shows some aircraft around an airport.

The rules regarding landing are as follows:

Rule 1: Any aircraft on a bearing on greater than 180° land first.
Rule 2: Aircraft on a bearing of 60° or less land second.
Rule 3: Aircraft at an altitude of 2000 m or more land last starting from lowest to highest altitude.

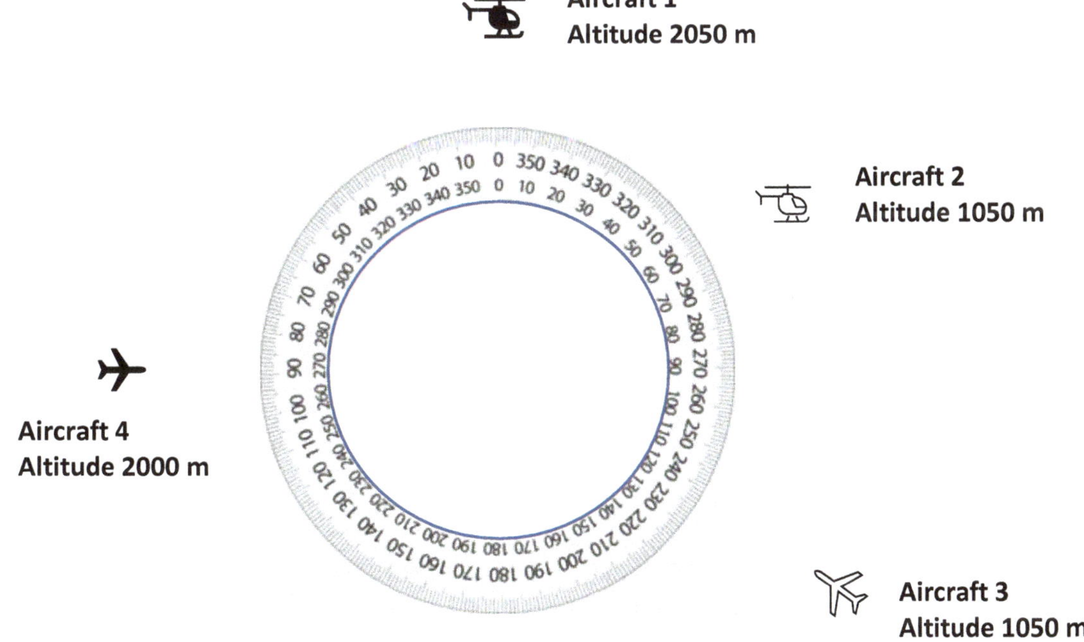

In what order do the aircraft land?

A 4 → 2 → 1 → 3

B 2 → 3 → 4 → 1

C 4 → 1 → 3 → 2

D 2 → 1 → 4 → 3

E 4 → 3 → 2 → 1

Question 34

Two cars are about to race round a single lap of a circuit as shown below. The length of the track is 4000 m.

The black car can cover 1 km in 20 seconds. The white car can cover 1 km in 22 seconds.

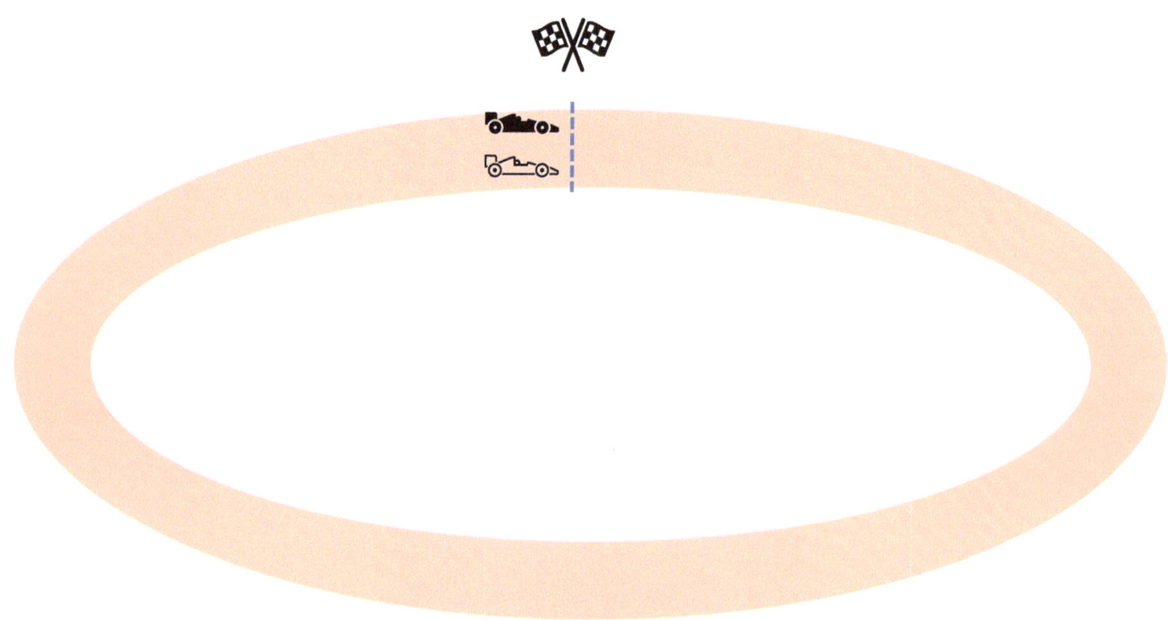

If they finish at exactly the same time, how much of a head start did the white car get?

A 100 m

B 1600 m

C 200 m

D 800 m

E 400 m

Question 35

Miles wants to buy some musical equipment for his band. The prices of equipment sets are shown below.

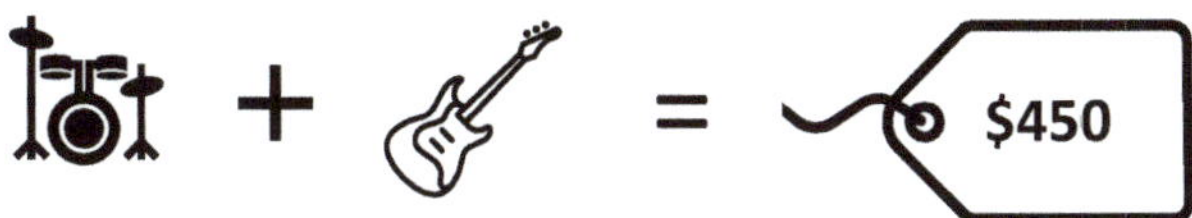

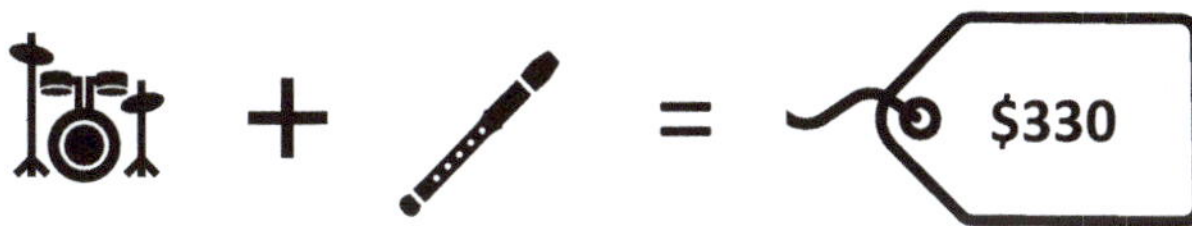

+ = $280

What would be the cost of this entire set?

+ + + = $?

A $730

B $610

C $880

D $530

E $780

Answers

Answers

Summary of Answers

1	D	8	B	15	C	22	C	29	B
2	A	9	C	16	A	23	E	30	C
3	B	10	A	17	B	24	C	31	D
4	C	11	E	18	E	25	D	32	A
5	D	12	D	19	D	26	A	33	B
6	D	13	E	20	A	27	E	34	E
7	E	14	D	21	B	28	B	35	A

A = 2, 10, 16, 20, 26, 32, 35

B = 3, 8, 17, 21, 28, 29, 33

C = 4, 9, 15, 22, 24, 30

D = 1, 5, 6, 12, 14, 19, 25, 31

E = 7, 11, 13, 18, 23, 27, 34

Fully worked solutions

Question 1

D

Davo's watch reads 21:48. Adding 45 minutes (three quarters of an hour) gives 22:33. In 12-hour format this must be after midday as the first two digits are greater than 12.

22:00 is 10 hours after 12:00 – hence the time is 10.33pm.

Question 2

A

Starting position:

Josephine then colours $\frac{2}{3}$ of the whole paper blue giving: (as 8 out of 12 is two-thirds)

There is only 1 section left to fill red.

Question 3

B

The smallest four-digit whole number is 1 000.

The largest four-digit whole number is 9 999.

Assume she misses a digit from the first number:
The digits that Serena can have missed may be either a 0 or 1 from the 1,000. If she misses the 1 then she is multiplying by zero and the answer is zero. Hence A can be obtained.

If Serena misses a zero then the number is 100 and the answer that can be obtained is 999 900 thus D can be obtained.

Assume she misses a digit from the second number:
This means the only digit that can be gone is a 9 thus the answer obtained will be 1 000 × 999 = 999 000 hence E can also be obtained.

Assume she misses a digit from EACH of the numbers:
In this scenario the second number becomes 999. The first one becomes 100 or 0.

Hence Serena can get 0 or 99 900 so C can also be obtained.

Hence B cannot be obtained.

Question 4

C

If the maximum speed would be 210 kilometres per hour, then each of the lines would be as follows:

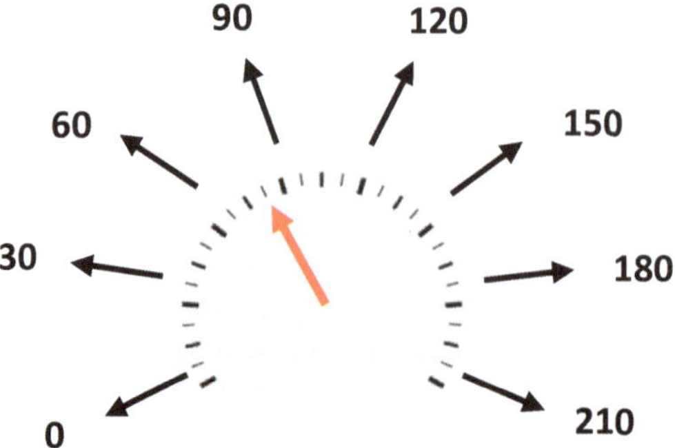

The answer is therefore C at 83 km per hour.

Question 5

D

17 hours ahead means that 8am on Tuesday in Los Angeles is 1am on Wednesday in Sydney (adding 17-hours to 8am).

The 10-hour sales will run from 1am Sydney time to 11am on Wednesday (Sydney time).

However, transaction must be commenced 10-minutes prior to it being completed and thus starting after 10.50am will be too late.

So, Almira can shop until 10.50am.

Question 6

D

cap + shirt = $30

trousers + shirt = $51

Adding the first of these together means that 2 shirts, a cap and a pair of trousers are collectively: $30 + $51 or $81.

However, we know this:

trousers + cap = $47

Hence 2 shirts must be $81 - $47 = $34. This means that each shirt is $17.

As each shirt is $17 then the cap must be $13 and the trousers $34.

Hence the price of the arrangement below MUST be: $34 + $17 + $13 = $64.

trousers + shirt + cap = $64

Answers

Question 7

E

In this code the 5th and 6th letters from the left indicate the year and month consecutively that the note was printed.

Hence the year denoted by the 5th letter (RED) is 2015 as: 2010 is A, so 2011 = B, 2012 = C, 2013 = D, 2014 = E and 2015 = F.

The month is denoted by the letter B (PURPLE) and is February. Hence E is correct.

05 BVIAF4BKNF
5
5 DOLLARS

Question 8

B

All of the words can be made except for the word "held", as no number can form the letter 'd' upside down. The 'b' in bless comes from the number 9.

Question 9

C

Clare's number is the largest even multiple of 3 less than 100 – which is 96.

Teresa's number is an even number which is the lowest multiple of 13 – which is 26.

The greatest difference is 96 − 26 = 70 or A.

Answers

Question 10

A

In the diagrams below A and B are squares. This means that the area of B must be 64 cm^2

because the side length of B is 8 cm (2 cm + 4 cm + 2 cm). So, the area of the left-hand shape must be 64 + 80 (20 cm × 4 cm) = 144 cm^2.

From the right-hand shape we know that the rectangular area is 22 cm × 2 cm = 44 cm^2. Hence square A must be 100 cm^2. Thus the side length of A must be 10 cm.

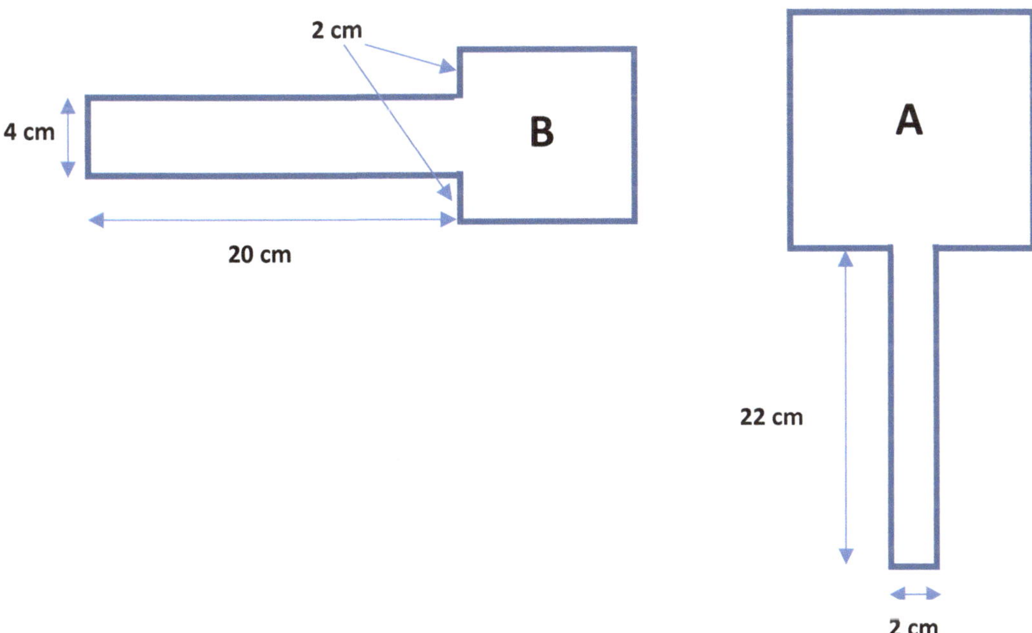

Question 11

E

Jessie and Joshua see this number: 12 430 000.

Joshua rounds the number to the nearest million making it 12 000 000.

Jessie rounds the number to the nearest hundred thousand making it 12 400 000.

The difference is 12 400 000 – 12 000 000 = 400 000 or E.

Question 12

D

Step 1:

Find the total that applies to each row, column and diagonal by adding 22 + 21 + 26 = 69.

Step 2:

We know that 22 + 24 + the number in the middle square (the diagonal) must add to 69.

Hence the middle number must be: 23.

22		★
21	23	
26		24

Total: 69

Step 3:

Finally, the other diagonal is 26 + 23 ★ = 69 so ★ must equal 20. Hence D is correct.

The complete square is shown below:

22	27	20
21	23	25
26	19	24

Question 13

E

If we add these two groups we see the following:

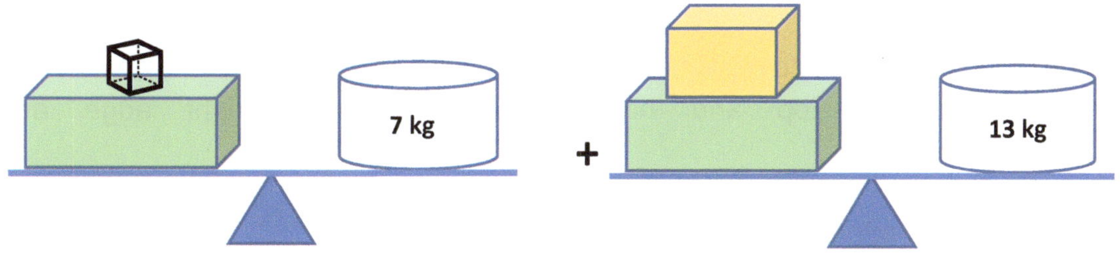

2 green boxes + the yellow box and the glass box collectively weigh 20 kg.

But we know from the below that the yellow box and the glass box weigh 10 kg combined.

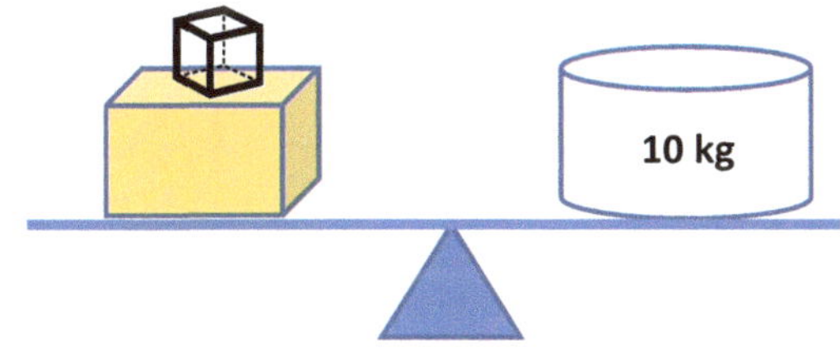

So, 2 green boxes MUST weigh 10 kg and therefore EACH green box weighs 5 kg.

We can now see that the glass box must weigh 2 kg and the yellow box 8 kg.

So, the arrangement below must be: 2 kg + 2 kg + 8 kg + 5 kg = 17 kg. Hence E is correct.

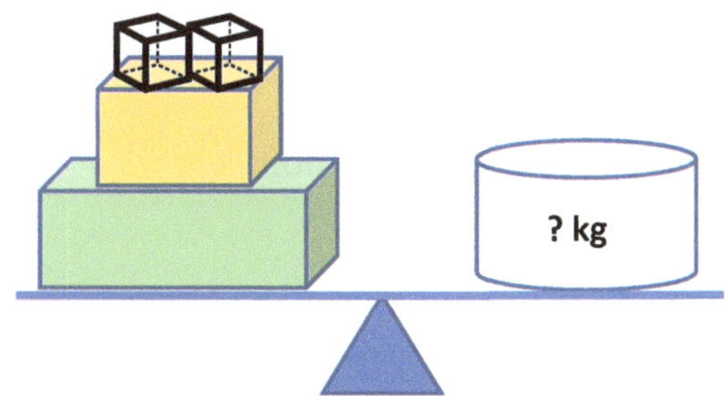

Question 14

D

The perimeter of X is 12 m + 8 m + 12 m + 8 m = 40 m. So the perimeter of Y must also be 40 m.

It should be evident that the red boundaries of shape Y equal 10 m. Hence, we know that these sides plus the top and bottom edges and the right edge are: 7 m + 7 m + 10 m = 24 m.

So, 24 m + 10 m (red edges) = 34 m.

Hence the last two lines must be 6 m meaning that a is 3 m. 3 m = 300 cm, hence D is correct.

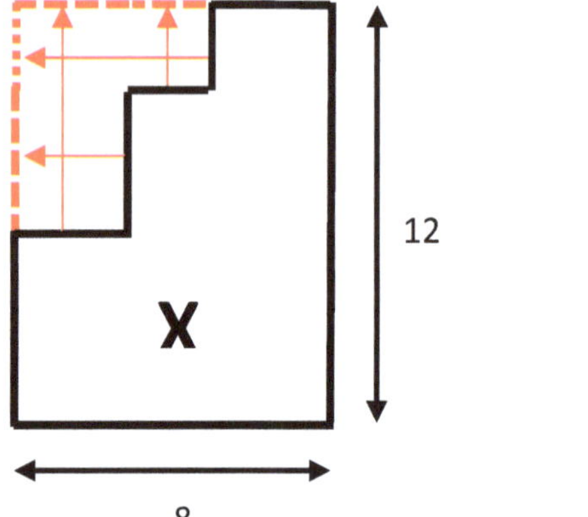

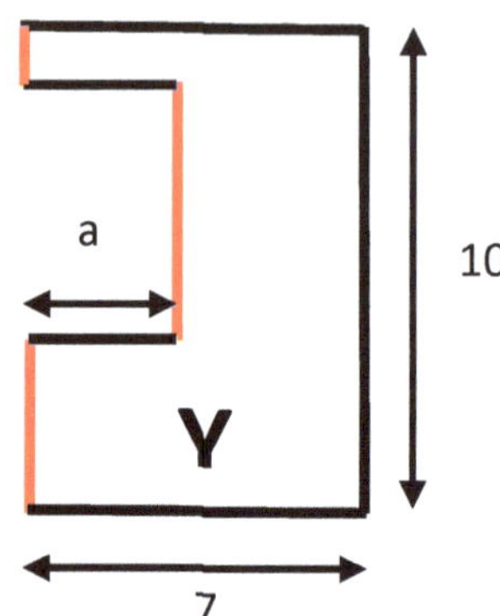

Question 15

C

Let the number of points for a heart sticker be equal to x. Let the number of points for a star sticker be equal to y

We can now say that $\mathbf{3x + 2y = 22}$ [as 3 heart stickers and 2 star stickers equal 22 points].

Similarly, $\mathbf{6x + 5y = 46}$ [as 6 heart stickers and 5 star stickers equal 26 points].

We can subtract the two equations to obtain the difference:

$$\mathbf{6x + 5y - (3x + 2y) = 46 - 22 = 24}$$

This means $\mathbf{3x + 3y = 24}$ [3 heart stickers and 3 star stickers must equal 24 points].

So, if this is the case then 1 heart sticker and 1 star must be $\frac{24}{3}$ = 8.

So, 2 heart stickers and 2 star stickers must collectively be worth 16 points.

Question 16

A

1 + 5 + A + 2 = B and 5 + A + 2 + B = 21

Substitute for B so:

5 + A + 2 + (1 + 5 + A + 2) = 21 [As we know that B = 1 + 5 + A + 2]

Therefore, 15 + 2A = 21

So, 2A = 21 – 15 = 6

Hence A = 3.

Also, since 5 + A + 2 + B = 21 then if A = 3 we have: 5 + 3 + 2 + B = 21

This means that 10 + B = 21 so B is equal to 11.

This means that C is 21 + 11 + 2 + 3 = 37.

Question 17

B

The multiples of 7 between 1 and 150 are:

7, 14, 21, 28, 35, 42, 49, 56, 63, 70, 77, 84, 91, 98, 105, 112, 119, 126, 133, 140, 147

Multiples of 3 are in **BLUE**

Multiples of 5 are **RED (noting that 105 is multiple of 3 and also 5)**

Multiples of 8 are in **PURPLE**

Hence there are 9 (7, 14, 28, 49, 77, 91, 98, 119, 133) so B is correct.

Answers

Question 18

E

There are:

9 faces

14 vertices or corners

21 edges

Total is 44

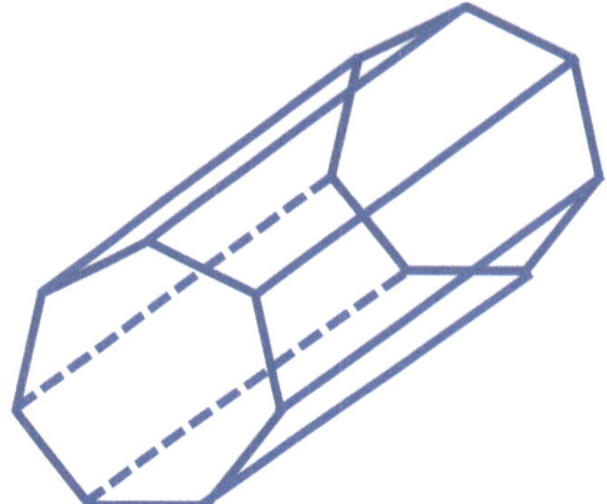

Question 19

D

Step 1

Find the common denominator for the fractions by finding the lowest common multiple, which is 36.

Josies eats $1\frac{1}{6}$ or $1\frac{6}{36}$

Mark eats $1\frac{1}{4}$ or $1\frac{9}{36}$

Edith eats $1\frac{2}{9}$ or $1\frac{8}{36}$

Clancy eats $\frac{3}{4}$ or $\frac{27}{36}$

Step 2

This all adds to give: $3 + \frac{6}{36} + \frac{9}{36} + \frac{8}{36} + \frac{27}{36} = 3 + \frac{50}{36} = 4\frac{14}{36} = 4\frac{7}{18}$

Step 3

The amount left is $6 - 4\frac{7}{18} = 1\frac{11}{18}$ for Gary to eat.

Question 20

A

There are 4 possible numbers that Huyen can get which when added to the 1 that Bao got will give a total greater than 2. These numbers are 2, 3 4 and 5. Hence the answer is $\frac{4}{8}$ which is also written as $\frac{1}{2}$.

Question 21

B

Statement 1 Angie went more than 13 metres under the surface of the water 3 times TRUE

Statement 2 Angie experienced a water temperature of 14 degrees 3 times TRUE

Statement 3 Angie spent most of her time less than 11 metres below the water's surface FALSE

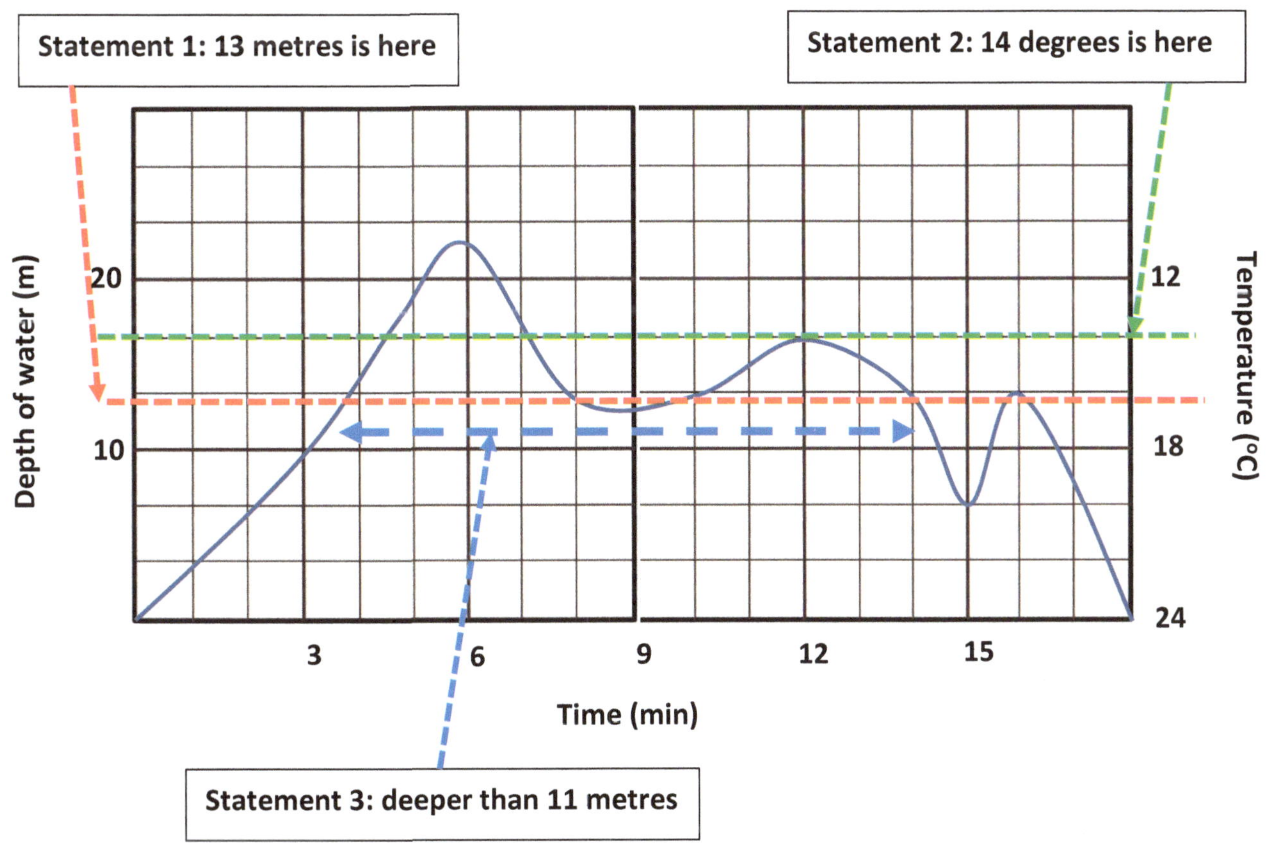

Question 22

C

The TWO axes of symmetry required – one vertical and one horizontal – are shown below:

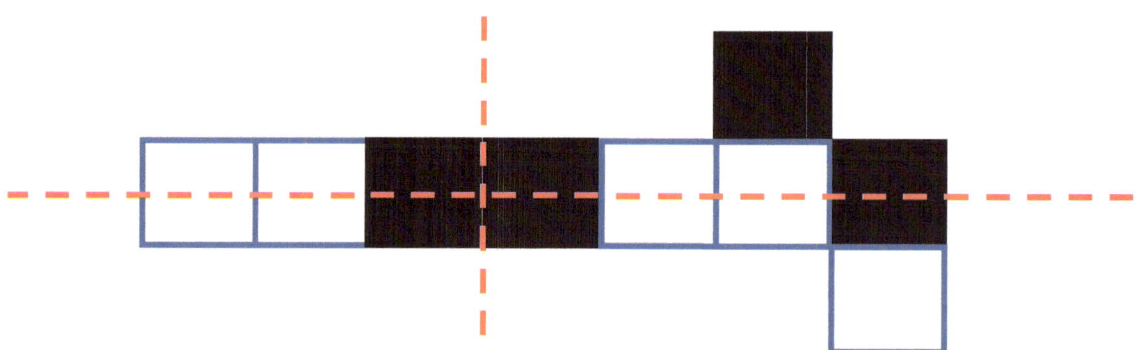

The squares needed are shown below:

Step 1: Add the FIRST white square and FIRST black square

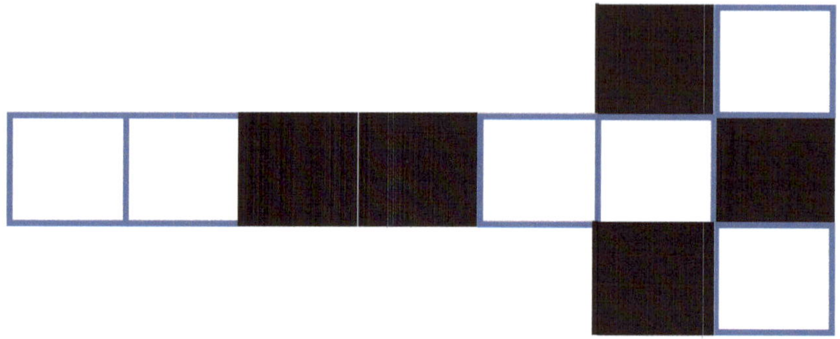

Step 2: Add the two white squares to the left

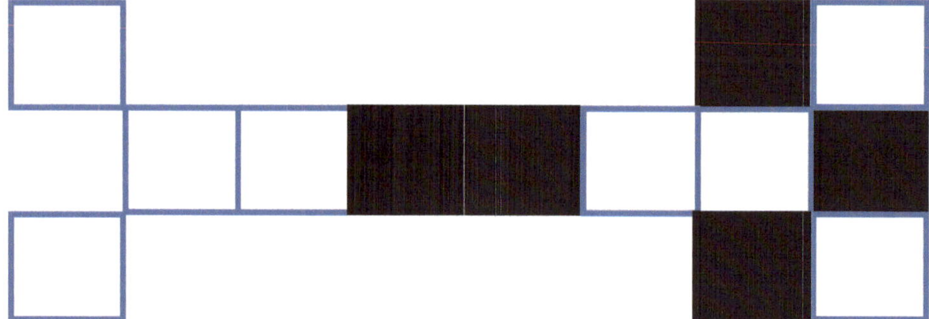

Answers

Step 3: Add the three black squares to the left

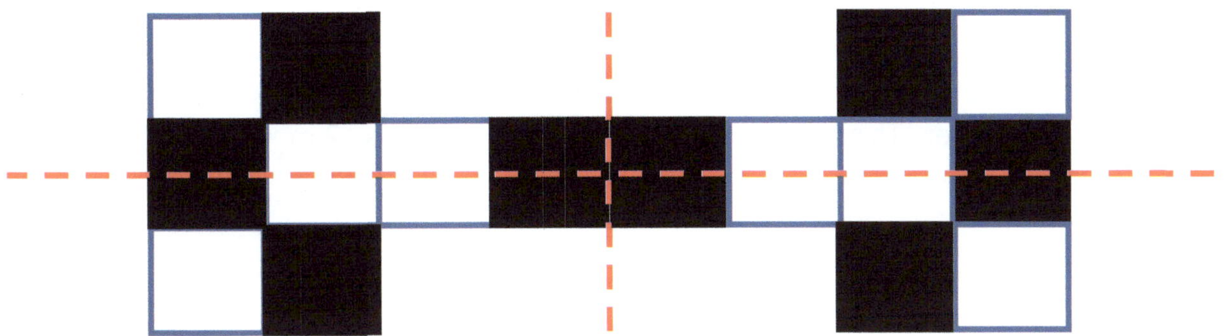

Thus 3 white squares and 4 black squares are required so Statements 3 and 4 are correct.

Question 23

E

Eight text messages are sent to each of 15 people is written as 8 × 15 or 15 × 8

Four people forward six of the messages to two other people is written: (4 × 6) × 2

Thus, the answer is: (15 × 8) + (6 × 4) × 2 as shown in E.

Question 24

C

Since the rectangle and the square have the same area the area of the rectangle must be 144 square metres. This is because the area of the square is 12 m × 12 m = 144 m^2.

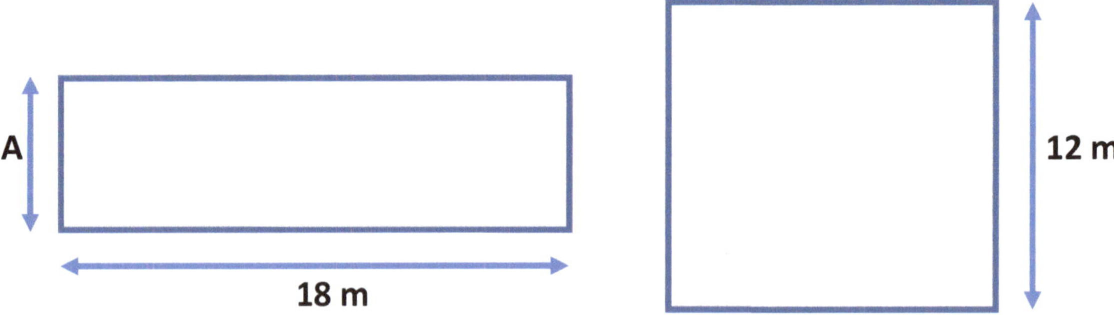

Hence, the value of A is calculated as follows: 18 × A = 144, so A = 8 m and the answer is C.

Question 25

D

The 2-litre bottle of orange juice contains 600 mL of juice.

Supriya adds a two-thirds of a small jug of water to the orange juice. The jug contains 600 mL when full. This means that 400 mL of water is added to the 600 mL of juice making it one litre or 1000 mL.

Since Supriya drinks 540 mL of the combined juice and water then there is 460 mL left.

She pours half of the rest into another bottle which means 230 mL is poured into the bottle.

Question 26

A

Since  × 13 = 104 then  = 8

And since  +  +  = 22

Then the value of  must be 7 and the answer is thus A.

Question 27

E

Lily had $14. She was given some money from Luisa. She then gave quarter of her money to Belinda. Belinda spent a quarter of this money and had $4.50 left.

How much did Lily give to Belinda?

A quarter of the money and she has $4.50 left. This means that $4.50 is three-quarters of her money. Thus, one quarter is $1.50. So, Belinda had $4.50 + $1.50 = $6.00. This is the amount that Lily gave her.

For completeness, $6.00 is a quarter of the money Lily had AFTER Luisa gave her money.

This means Lily had $24 as Luisa gave her $10.

Question 28

B

There are 20 shirts in the box and the chance of picking an orange shirt is 0.2. This means that there must be 0.2 × 20 = 4 orange shirts in the box.

The chance of picking a purple shirt is 0.15 thus there must be 0.15 × 20 = 3 purple shirts.

We are told there is one black shirt.

So, there are 12 shirts whose colour has to be determined. The ratio of blue shirts to white shirts is 5:1. This means that in a pile of 6 blue shirts and white shirts, 5 of the shirts will be blue and 1 will be white.

So, we now know that of the 12 remaining shirts 10 are blue and 2 are white, hence B.

Question 29

B

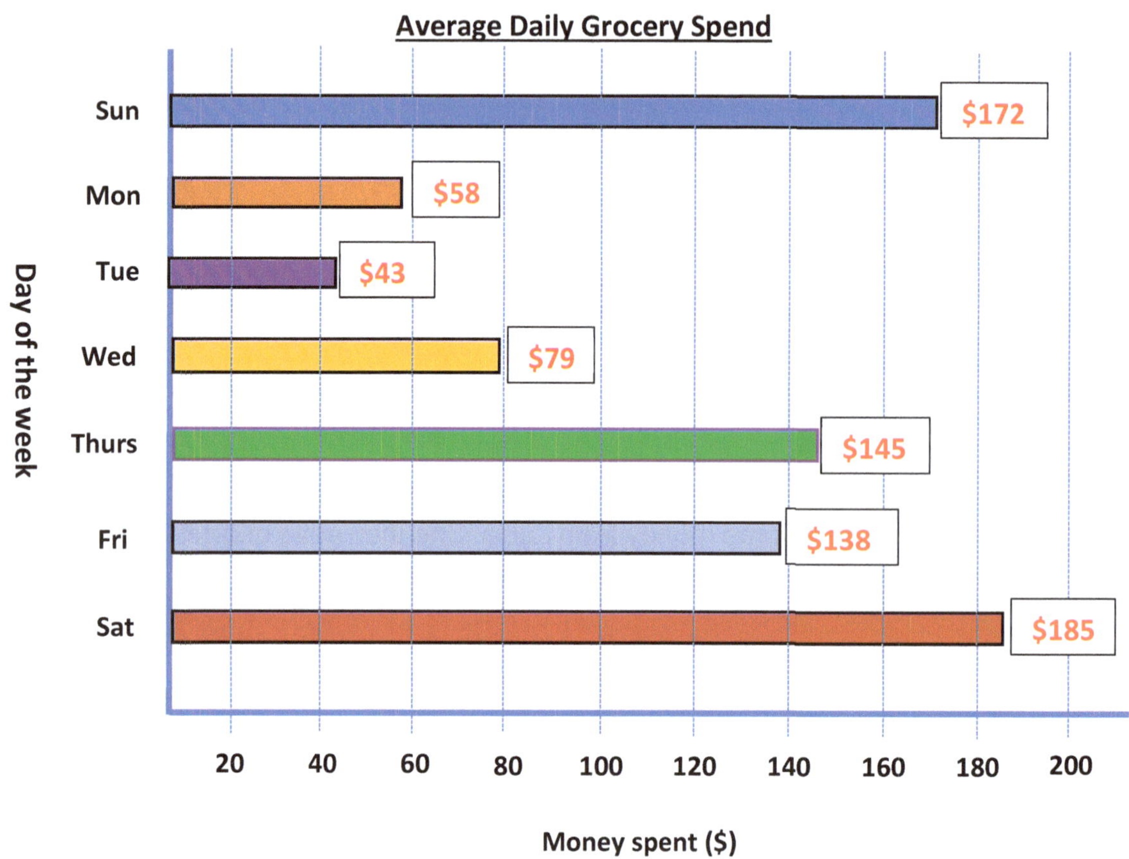

Statement 1

On average people spent twice as much on Thursday than on Wednesday. FALSE

Statement 2

The average spending on Sunday is four times the average Tuesday spending. TRUE

Statement 3

The average weekend spending is greater than the all the other days together. FALSE

Hence only Statement 2 is true - which is B.

Question 30

C

We know that Jake eats 5 slices, Darcy and Chan 2 each. This makes a total of 9 slices.

We also know that $\frac{1}{3}$ of the slices go to Andrew and $\frac{1}{6}$ to Boris. The sum of these fractions is $\frac{1}{2}$. Hence, half is left which is the 9 slices that went to Jake, Darcy and Chan.

The total number of slices must be 18.

Boris, who ate $\frac{1}{6}$ must have eaten three slices. Hence C is correct.

Question 31

D

A is the white square within the black rectangle and its area is 2 m × 2 m = 4 m^2.

The white rectangle has dimensions of 6 m × 2 m = 12 m^2.

The total cut out is 4 m^2 + 12 m^2 = 16m^2.

The black rectangle has dimensions 12 m × 5 m so it would have had an area of 60 m^2.

With the white pieces cut out the remaining area is 60 m^2 – 16 m^2 = 44 m^2. Hence D is correct.

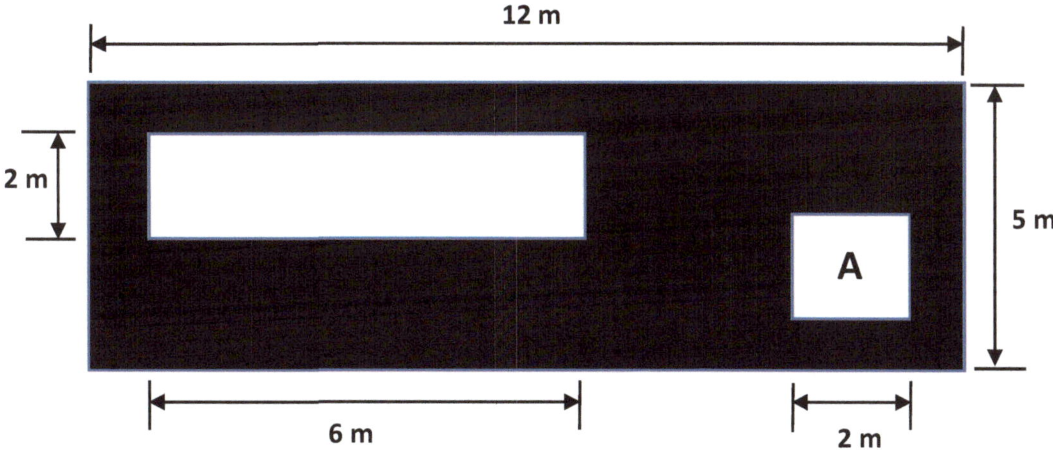

Question 32

A

As Queenie is using the scale on the right-hand side ONLY.

She fills the jug to 75 mL of lemon juice.

She then adds water taking the mix to 325 mL.

She then adds orange juice to bring it to the fourth line from the top of the scale.

She pours half of this mix into a glass.

How much orange juice is in the glass?

When Queenie adds water to the 75 mL of lemon juice the volume goes up to 325 mL. By adding orange juice, it goes up to the 4th line from the top of the scale which is 425 mL. This means Queenie added 100 mL of orange juice to the mix.

If she pours half of this into a glass, there must be 50 mL of orange juice in the glass. Hence the answer is A.

Answers

Question 33

B

Rule 1: Any aircraft on a bearing on greater than 180° land first.
Rule 2: Aircraft on a bearing of 60° or less land second.
Rule 3: Aircraft at an altitude of 2000 m or more land last starting from lowest to highest altitude.

According to Rule 1, Aircraft 4 would land first as its bearing is 270°, BUT Rule 1 is subject to Rule 3 thus Aircraft 4 cannot be first. So, we go to Rule 2. This affects Aircraft 1 and 2, however Aircraft 1 is also at an altitude affected by Rule 3 so the LAST two aircraft to land must be 4 then 1.

So, Aircraft 2 must be first to land, followed by Aircraft 3 then Aircraft 4 then Aircraft 1 as shown in B.

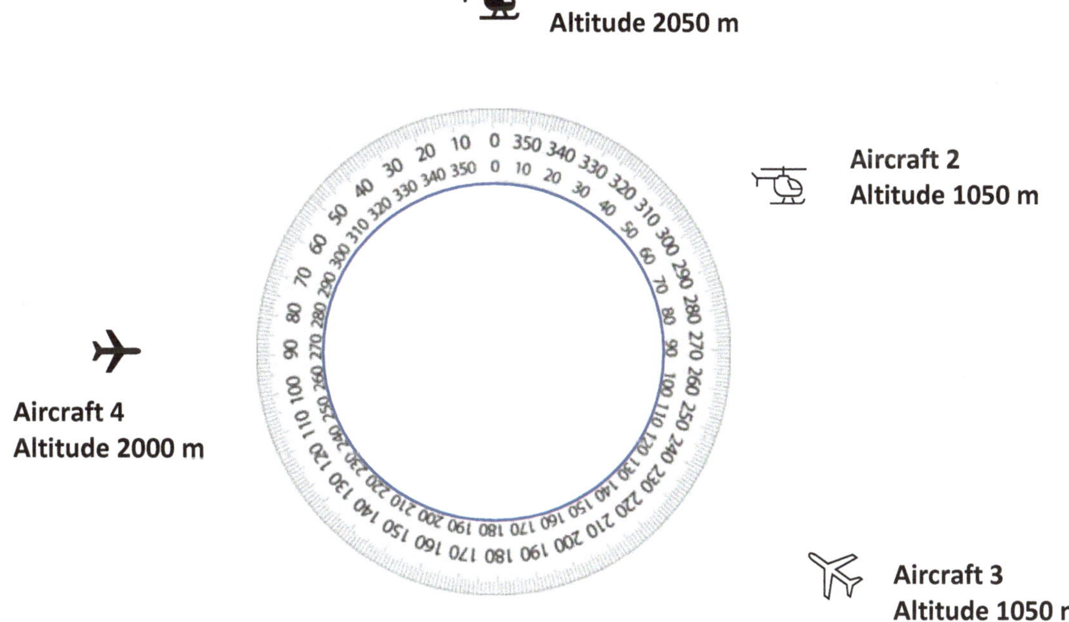

Question 34

E

The black car can cover 1 km in 20 seconds. The white car can cover 1 km in 22 seconds. This means that if they had started at the same time, then the black car would finish 8 seconds ahead (2 seconds/kilometre × 4 kilometres = 8 seconds).

8 seconds for the black car would mean it would cover 8/20 of a kilometre = 400 m.

The white car would therefore need to be given a 400-metre head start for them to finish at exactly the same time. Hence E is correct.

Question 35

A

Adding the first two sets gives:

drum set + guitar = $450
drum set + recorder = $330

Add to give $780

Subtracting this from the total:

guitar + recorder = $280

So, \$780 – \$280 = \$500 meaning that 2 drum sets cost \$500. Hence each drum set is \$250.

This means that a guitar cost $200 (from the first picture above).

From the second picture we know that a recorder must cost \$330 – \$250 = \$80

Hence the cost of this set must be:

drum set + recorder + guitar + guitar = $?

\$250 + \$80 + \$200 + \$200 = \$730 which is A.

Mathematical Reasoning

FOR SELECTIVE SCHOOL TESTS,
OPPORTUNITY CLASS TEST
AND PROBLEM SOLVING

Use pencil when filling out this sheet

Fill in the circle correctly				
●	(B)	(C)	(D)	(E)

If you make a mistake neatly cross it out and circle the correct response				
☒	●	(C)	(D)	(E)

MULTIPLE CHOICE ANSWER SHEET

1	(A)	(B)	(C)	(D)	(E)	19	(A)	(B)	(C)	(D)	(E)
2	(A)	(B)	(C)	(D)	(E)	20	(A)	(B)	(C)	(D)	(E)
3	(A)	(B)	(C)	(D)	(E)	21	(A)	(B)	(C)	(D)	(E)
4	(A)	(B)	(C)	(D)	(E)	22	(A)	(B)	(C)	(D)	(E)
5	(A)	(B)	(C)	(D)	(E)	23	(A)	(B)	(C)	(D)	(E)
6	(A)	(B)	(C)	(D)	(E)	24	(A)	(B)	(C)	(D)	(E)
7	(A)	(B)	(C)	(D)	(E)	25	(A)	(B)	(C)	(D)	(E)
8	(A)	(B)	(C)	(D)	(E)	26	(A)	(B)	(C)	(D)	(E)
9	(A)	(B)	(C)	(D)	(E)	27	(A)	(B)	(C)	(D)	(E)
10	(A)	(B)	(C)	(D)	(E)	28	(A)	(B)	(C)	(D)	(E)
11	(A)	(B)	(C)	(D)	(E)	29	(A)	(B)	(C)	(D)	(E)
12	(A)	(B)	(C)	(D)	(E)	30	(A)	(B)	(C)	(D)	(E)
13	(A)	(B)	(C)	(D)	(E)	31	(A)	(B)	(C)	(D)	(E)
14	(A)	(B)	(C)	(D)	(E)	32	(A)	(B)	(C)	(D)	(E)
15	(A)	(B)	(C)	(D)	(E)	33	(A)	(B)	(C)	(D)	(E)
16	(A)	(B)	(C)	(D)	(E)	34	(A)	(B)	(C)	(D)	(E)
17	(A)	(B)	(C)	(D)	(E)	35	(A)	(B)	(C)	(D)	(E)
18	(A)	(B)	(C)	(D)	(E)						

Mathematical Reasoning

FOR SELECTIVE SCHOOL TESTS,
OPPORTUNITY CLASS TEST
AND PROBLEM SOLVING

Use pencil when filling out this sheet

Fill in the circle correctly				
●	B	C	D	E

If you make a mistake neatly cross it out and circle the correct response				
● (crossed out)	●	C	D	E

MULTIPLE CHOICE ANSWER SHEET

1	A	B	C	D	E	19	A	B	C	D	E
2	A	B	C	D	E	20	A	B	C	D	E
3	A	B	C	D	E	21	A	B	C	D	E
4	A	B	C	D	E	22	A	B	C	D	E
5	A	B	C	D	E	23	A	B	C	D	E
6	A	B	C	D	E	24	A	B	C	D	E
7	A	B	C	D	E	25	A	B	C	D	E
8	A	B	C	D	E	26	A	B	C	D	E
9	A	B	C	D	E	27	A	B	C	D	E
10	A	B	C	D	E	28	A	B	C	D	E
11	A	B	C	D	E	29	A	B	C	D	E
12	A	B	C	D	E	30	A	B	C	D	E
13	A	B	C	D	E	31	A	B	C	D	E
14	A	B	C	D	E	32	A	B	C	D	E
15	A	B	C	D	E	33	A	B	C	D	E
16	A	B	C	D	E	34	A	B	C	D	E
17	A	B	C	D	E	35	A	B	C	D	E
18	A	B	C	D	E						

Mathematical Reasoning

FOR SELECTIVE SCHOOL TESTS, OPPORTUNITY CLASS TEST AND PROBLEM SOLVING

Use pencil when filling out this sheet

Fill in the circle correctly				
●	B	C	D	E

If you make a mistake neatly cross it out and circle the correct response				
✗	●	C	D	E

MULTIPLE CHOICE ANSWER SHEET

1	A	B	C	D	E	19	A	B	C	D	E
2	A	B	C	D	E	20	A	B	C	D	E
3	A	B	C	D	E	21	A	B	C	D	E
4	A	B	C	D	E	22	A	B	C	D	E
5	A	B	C	D	E	23	A	B	C	D	E
6	A	B	C	D	E	24	A	B	C	D	E
7	A	B	C	D	E	25	A	B	C	D	E
8	A	B	C	D	E	26	A	B	C	D	E
9	A	B	C	D	E	27	A	B	C	D	E
10	A	B	C	D	E	28	A	B	C	D	E
11	A	B	C	D	E	29	A	B	C	D	E
12	A	B	C	D	E	30	A	B	C	D	E
13	A	B	C	D	E	31	A	B	C	D	E
14	A	B	C	D	E	32	A	B	C	D	E
15	A	B	C	D	E	33	A	B	C	D	E
16	A	B	C	D	E	34	A	B	C	D	E
17	A	B	C	D	E	35	A	B	C	D	E
18	A	B	C	D	E						